Investigating STORMS

Debra J. Housel, M.S.Ed.

Earth and Space Science Readers:

Investigating Storms

Publishing Credits

Editorial Director
Dona Herweck Rice

Associate Editor
Joshua BishopRoby

Editor-in-Chief
Sharon Coan, M.S.Ed.

Creative Director
Lee Aucoin

Illustration Manager
Timothy J. Bradley

Publisher
Rachelle Cracchiolo, M.S.Ed

Science Contributor
Sally Ride Science

Science Consultants
Scott Hetsko,
Chief Meteorologist at
WROC-TV, Rochester, New York
Nancy McKeown,
Planetary Geologist
William B. Rice,
Engineering Geologist

Teacher Created Materials
5301 Oceanus Drive
Huntington Beach, CA 92649-1030
http://www.tcmpub.com
ISBN 978-0-7439-0551-0

Printed in China
Nordica.082019.CA21901409

Table of Contents

Water and Wind

You're looking forward to a weekend full of sunshine. You check the news, just to be sure the skies will be clear. The weather report says a storm is on the way. How do they know? The skies look clear and sunny. How can they tell that rain is coming?

Rain is one kind of **precipitation** (pri-sip-i-TEY-shuhn). Precipitation is any form of water falling from the sky. It can be frozen like snow or liquid like rain. First, the water has to get into the air, though. Then, something has to make it come down again. What happens to make it rain?

The sun heats the water on Earth's surface. This makes water **evaporate** (i-VAP-uh-reyt) from lakes, rivers, oceans, and the ground. This water turns into vapor, or a gas. It rises into the air and cools. It **condenses** (kuhn-DENS-es) and forms clouds. Eventually, some of the cloud drops get so big and heavy that they fall back to the earth. They come as rain, snow, sleet, freezing rain, or hail.

snowflakes

raindrops

Raindrops are small groups of water molecules and dust. When they get too heavy to stay inside a cloud, they fall. When it's really cold, raindrops can freeze and become sleet, or they can become ice crystals. These crystals group together to become snowflakes.

When water vapor strikes a freezing surface, it looks like snow, but it has a special name. It is called frost.

No matter the name, water from the sky is always the same thing. It is precipitation.

frost

Rain, Rain Go Away

Think it rains too much where you live? Try being on the windward side of Mount Waialeale (wy-ah-LAY-ah-lay) on the island of Kauai in Hawaii. Its average rainfall is 12 meters (39 feet) per year!

Freezing rain falls just as rain and then enters colder air. It's not in the cold air long enough to freeze. It just becomes super cooled, almost to freezing. Then, the raindrops freeze as soon as they touch a surface.

Sometimes, raindrops freeze into chunks. These chunks are called hail. This happens when raindrops get caught in a cloud's updraft. An updraft is a stream of air that moves upward. When this happens, the raindrops become large ice pellets.

Wind is also a part of storms. Wind is moving air. Air is heavy. It pushes down on the ground beneath it. This creates pressure. Wind is air that blows from a high-pressure area to a low-pressure area. The greater the difference in air pressure, the faster the wind moves. This air pressure is measured with a **barometer** (buh-ROM-i-ter).

barometer

Human Hailstones

The size of hail depends on how many times the ice pellets cycle through the cloud due to the updraft and gravity. The stronger the updraft, the bigger the hailstone gets. The biggest ones can ruin crops, kill animals, and dent cars.

Sometimes hail forms around objects already in the air. In the 1930s, three men became human hailstones! They had parachuted out of gliders because of a storm. Their parachutes caught updrafts. This pulled them up into the clouds. Water froze all around them. The men went up and down many times. They became large hailstones. Then, they fell from the sky. Amazingly, one man actually survived.

hailstones the size of golf balls

Thunderstorms

A storm that has thunder and lightning is called a thunderstorm. A thunderstorm can be very powerful. At any moment there are about 2,000 thunderstorms happening on Earth. There are 100 lightning strikes per second. A 20-minute thunderstorm drops 473 million liters (125 million gallons) of water. It gives off more electrical (i-LEK-tri-kuhl) energy than is used in Beijing, China, in a whole week!

Thunderstorms usually happen in warm, humid weather. They happen when warm and cold **fronts** meet. A front is a boundary between masses of air. The cold air mass slides under the warm air mass.

Watch Out!

The Eiffel Tower in Paris gets struck by lightning dozens of times each year.

Warm air is lighter than cold air. It rises up in the sky. A thunderstorm begins when strong **currents** of air move upward in the clouds. This air causes the cloud to swell. These swollen clouds are called **thunderheads**. Some thunderheads can be up to 15,000 meters (12 miles) tall. As raindrops form, winds swirl them around within the cloud.

Lightning crashes over Tucson, Arizona.

Ancient Wisdom

For hundreds of years, American Indian tribes living near cedar trees have known to use them during thunderstorms. The people would throw bits of cedar into their fires when lightning was near. The reasons for this are in chemistry (KEM-uh-stree), although the people did not know it. Cedar wood has a negative electric charge. This repels the electric charge of the lightning. It kept their homes safe from lightning strikes.

Inside the thunderhead, electrical energy builds. The cloud cannot hold all the electricity (i-lek-TRIS-i-tee). The electricity is released from the cloud as lightning bolts. Lightning heats the surrounding air instantly. It actually makes the air hotter than the surface of the sun.

The hot air expands so fast that it breaks the speed of sound. This causes a booming sound that we call thunder. Thunder and lightning happen at the same time. You see the flash first because light travels much faster than sound.

Lightning can be dangerous. If it hits trees or buildings, they can catch fire. If it strikes people or animals, they may die. Never take shelter under a tree. If a bolt hits the tree, the electricity can move from it to you!

Sand thick as fog storms through Beijing, China.

Sandstorms

In 1968, a sandstorm showered England with red dust. A large weather system had come from Africa, carrying the dust. It fell on England as red rain!

A sandstorm is a strong, dry wind full of dust. Sandstorms form as wind rushes over a desert. The wind picks up sand. The air becomes thick with dust and sand. Sometimes the dust is so thick that you can't even see your hand in front of your face. It can be hard to breathe in a sandstorm. The winds are strong enough to move sand dunes and destroy roads.

Tornadoes and Waterspouts

A tornado acts like a gigantic vacuum cleaner. It roars along at a speed of about 50 kilometers (30 miles) per hour. It smashes everything in its path. It can even lift cars into the air, dropping them far away.

Tornadoes can happen anywhere. The central states in the United States have more tornadoes than anywhere else on Earth. Each year about 1,000 tornadoes occur. Luckily, most are weak. Others are strong. They can do a great deal of damage.

Tornadoes can begin as thunderstorms. Thunderstorms can form **supercells**. A supercell is a large thunderstorm that rotates. A supercell can be very dangerous. Supercells can cause hail, damaging winds, and tornadoes.

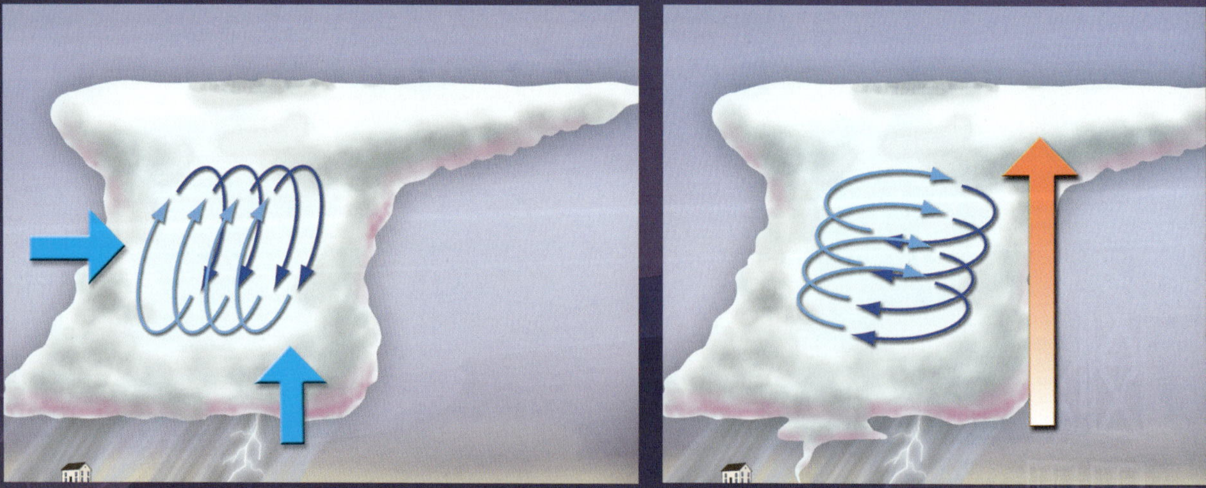

A thunderstorm can develop a supercell inside it. Winds go up, over, down, and back in a circle.

The supercell can get tilted up and down by a strong updraft.

A supercell forms when strong winds blow in opposite directions. This starts the air within a thunderhead to spin. If it touches the ground, it becomes a tornado.

Fujita Tornado Scale

Tetsuya Theodore Fujita made a scale in 1971. This scale is used to rate the power of a tornado. Here is part of the Fujita Scale:

Rank	Strength	Speed
F0–F1	Weak	winds 64–180 km/h (40–112 mph)
F2–F3	Strong	winds 181–332 km/h (113–206 mph)
F4–F5	Violent	winds over 333 km/h (207+ mph)

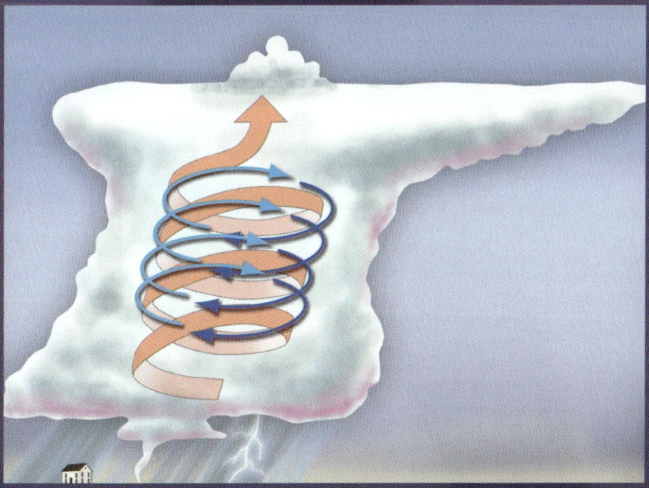

If the vertical supercell keeps going, it starts sucking wind and everything else up the cell. A tornado is born.

Terrible Twister

The deadliest tornado ever recorded struck on March 18, 1925. It started in Missouri and traveled for more than 350 kilometers (219 miles). It lasted over three and a half hours. It hit Illinois and Indiana, too. It left 689 dead, 2,000 hurt, and 11,000 homeless.

Doppler radar station

People used to be at the mercy of these storms. Now there is some advance warning. **Doppler (DAWP-ler) radar** can detect when such a storm is forming. Then the government issues a tornado watch. If a tornado touches down, the watch turns into a warning. If this happens, people should take cover in a basement or a storm shelter. The only safe place to be during a violent tornado is underground.

storm cellar

Raining Fish and Frogs

Compared to tornadoes, waterspouts are smaller and have slower winds. Waterspouts suck up things from the water. Then they drop them on land. In this way, fish have fallen in Mexico, frogs in France, and tadpoles in Canada! Most of the time, waterspouts drop things close by the source. In 1988, hundreds of small pink frogs from Africa rained down on a British village. Strong updrafts kept the frogs in the air long enough to cross the sea.

Hurricanes

As bad as tornadoes are, they aren't the worst storms. Each year hurricanes cause more damage than all other storms combined. Why? Hurricanes are huge, and they last a long time.

Hurricanes start as tropical storms. They form in late summer or fall over warm water. The center of a hurricane is called the eye. It has very low pressure. Clouds rush toward it. But they start to spin due to Earth's rotation. As a result, the eye stays calm. It has no clouds and no wind. When people talk about the calm in the eye of the storm, that's what they mean.

Storm Scale

In 1969, two scientists developed the Saffir-Simpson Scale for Tropical Storms to classify them.

Category	Wind Speed
1	119–153 km/h (74–95 mph)
2	154–177 km/h (96–110 mph)
3	178–209 km/h (111–130 mph)
4	210–249 km/h (131–155 mph)
5	251 km/h (156 mph) or higher

In this satellite image of a hurricane, the eye can be seen clearly.

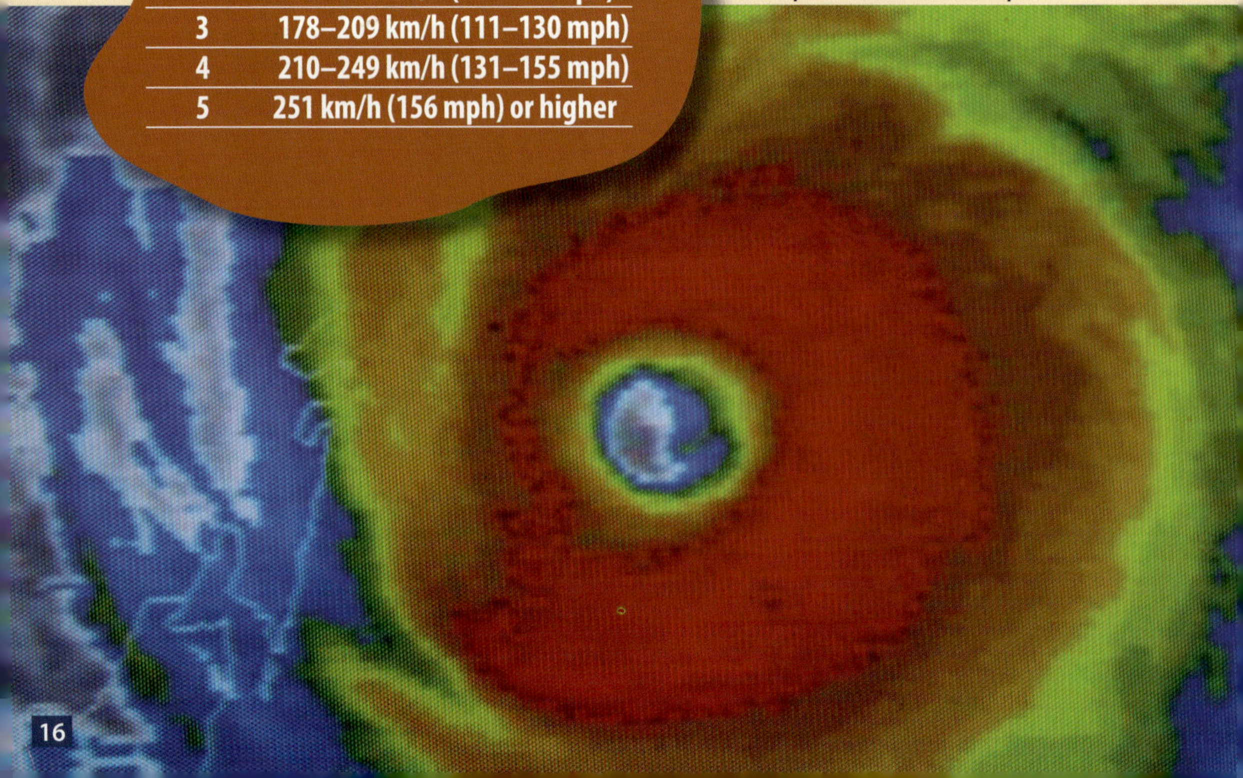

When a storm's winds reach 63 kilometers (39 miles) per hour, it is called a tropical storm. As a tropical storm spins across the ocean, it picks up more moisture. If the winds reach 119 kilometers (74 miles) per hour, it's a hurricane. By the time it reaches shore, the storm may be 805 kilometers (500 miles) wide with wind speeds of 241 kilometers (150 miles) per hour.

Record-Breaking Hurricanes

One of the worst storms on record is Hurricane Mitch. It struck Honduras, Nicaragua, and the United States in 1998. Thousands of people were killed, and thousands more were missing. One of the most destructive hurricanes was Hurricane Andrew in 1992. It raged for twelve days. It struck the Bahamas and the United States, causing more than $25 billion in property damages.

destruction caused by a hurricane

These pedestrians battle the powerful winds of Hurricane Katrina as it crosses Florida in August 2005.

High winds are not the only problem. The storm pushes water in front of it. As this water reaches land, it piles up in a wave called a **storm surge**. This causes huge flooding. The water level rises. Small buildings near the shore are suddenly underwater. Then, the water recedes. It pulls things like cars and homes out to sea.

Hurricanes also strike Australia, where they are called willy-willies. When they hit Asia, they are called typhoons. Cyclones form in the Indian Ocean. No matter what they are called, they act the same. These storms gather water from the sea. Then, they dump it on land. Strangely, the water they drop isn't salty like sea water. That is because when the ocean water evaporates, it leaves its salt behind.

When it suddenly stops raining, becomes very calm, and the sun shines, you may think it's all over. But this is just the eye of the storm. The other side of the storm is about to hit! Hurricanes slowly die as they move inland. They leave tremendous damage in their wake.

Floods are a terrible result of hurricanes.

Naming Hurricanes

Scientists name hurricanes in the Atlantic Ocean by using six lists of 21 names each. They switch to a new list each year. Boy and girl names alternate from A to W, skipping Q and U. If all 21 names are used, the Greek alphabet names the rest. This happened for the first time in 2005. There were a record number of hurricanes.

So, what sort of names are picked? Here is the list for the year 2005: Arlene, Bret, Cindy, Dennis, Emily, Franklin, Gert, Harvey, Irene, Jose, Katrina, Lee, Maria, Nate, Ophelia, Philippe, Rita, Stan, Tammy, Vince, Wilma, Alpha, Beta, Gamma, Delta, Epsilon, and Zeta.

Hurricane Rita from 2005

Blizzards

Ice, snow, wind, and freezing temperatures (TEM-per-uh-chers) can combine to create terrible, deadly storms. These storms happen in the winter. The worst are called blizzards.

Blizzards have heavy snowfall, high winds, and extremely low temperatures. The wind combines with the cold temperature. This causes a dangerous condition called wind chill. Wind chill means that the air feels colder to living things than it actually is. The faster the wind blows, the faster people lose body heat. Wind chill causes people and animals to get hypothermia (hahy-puh-THUR-mee-uh) and freeze to death. Hypothermia is when the body's temperature drops too low to survive.

Wind chill or just very cold temperatures can cause frostbite. A person's ears, nose, cheeks, toes, and fingers can get so cold that the blood stops flowing through them. Severely frostbitten body parts may die and then must be removed.

Blizzards can occur anywhere that it snows. They are most likely to happen in northern Europe, Canada, Russia, and the United States. Blizzards are also found in parts of South America. These storms often form after a spell of warm weather. When very cold air meets warm, moist air, a blizzard may be born.

The Storms of the Centuries

A blizzard in 1888 lasted nearly 24 hours. It killed 400 people. It dumped 53 centimeters (21 inches) of snow on New York City. Snow buried homes. People dug tunnels to get out. No one could get in or out of the city for a week.

One of the worst blizzards ever was in March 1993. It raged all the way from Alabama to Massachusetts in the United States and eastern Canada. Along the way, it broke records for low pressure, wind speed, low temperatures, and snowfall. Strong wind gusts turned into tornadoes. Over 270 people were killed.

Years ago, there was no warning system for blizzards. People often were taken by surprise and sometimes were caught in the storm. Even so, many people had to go outside to do chores. They had to get to their barns to care for their animals. To keep from getting

lost in case of a blizzard, they tied a rope from their home to the barn. They held onto it as they walked.

Blizzards often stop travel. They make it impossible for people to see where they're going. Roads and runways are slippery. Travel by road or air often comes to a halt.

In January 2006, one of the worst blizzards in recorded history struck parts of China and Japan. It lasted for nine days. It dumped snow up to 3 meters (10 feet) high. Some homes were not built for such heavy snowfall and collapsed under the weight.

It takes a lot of work to clean up after a blizzard!

Survivor Story

In February 2001, a toddler nearly froze to death in Canada. In the middle of the night, she wandered out of the house. Her mother found her in the snow at 3 A.M. and quickly called the ambulance. The little girl's toes had frozen together. Her mouth was frozen shut. Doctors had trouble giving her a breathing tube. Her heart had stopped beating. The doctors slowly warmed her up. Then, the girl's heart started beating again. Today she lives a normal life. The cold temperature actually helped her brain to stay alive.

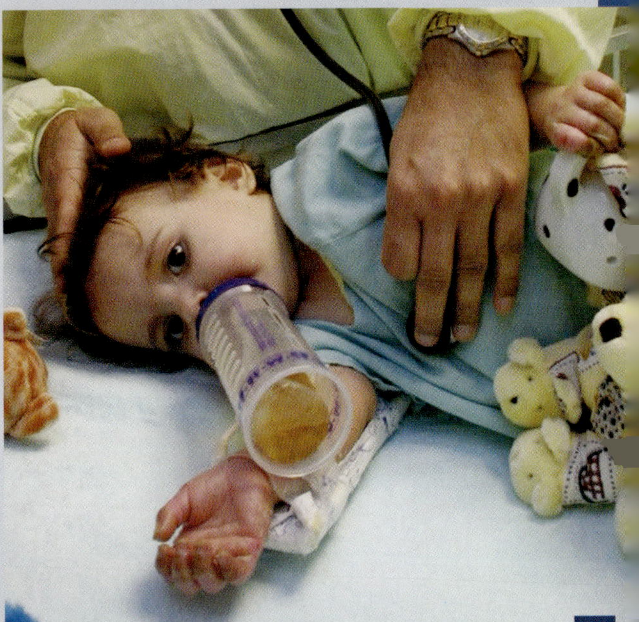

Jet Streams and Ocean Currents

All weather happens in the layer of atmosphere closest to Earth's surface. Many things affect weather. The biggest factors are heat, water, and wind.

The sun warms Earth's surface. This makes heat and water rise into the atmosphere. There are four main jet streams there, high in the sky. Jet streams are rivers of wind. They lower the heat and move around the moisture. They blow an average of 200 kilometers per hour (125 miles per hour).

Jet streams are one of the driving forces of weather changes. They are thousands of miles long, hundreds of miles wide, and several miles deep. They bend and move in different ways. They don't always stay in the same spot. They move either toward the equator or away from it.

Fighter pilots discovered jet streams during World War II when they had trouble flying against headwinds.

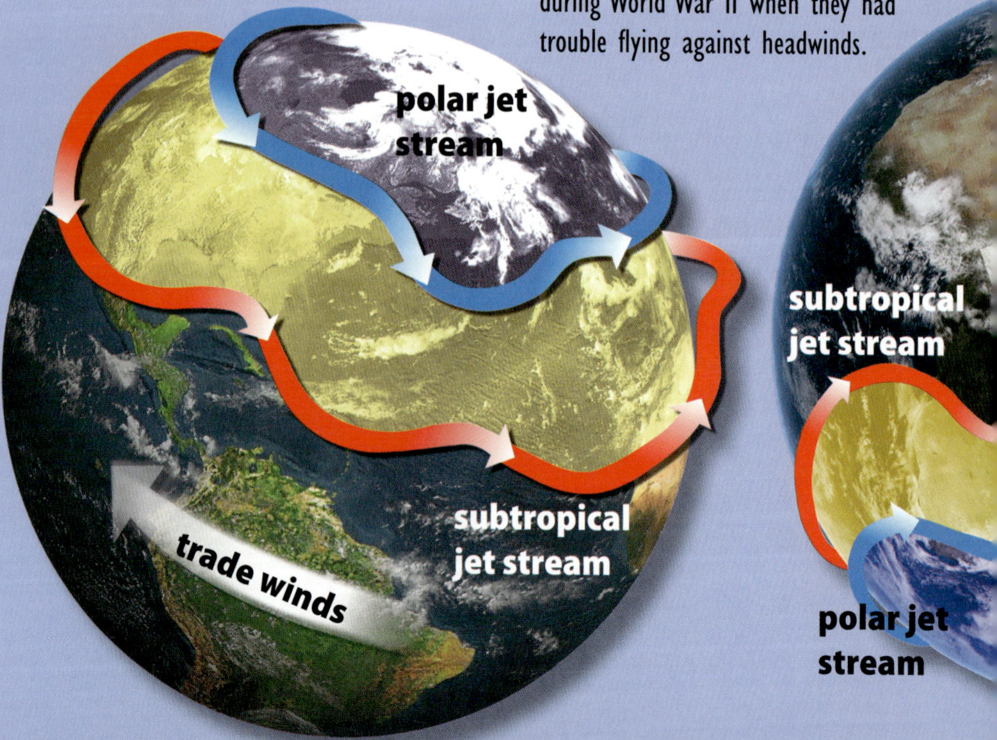

glacier

jet stream as it appears in both hemispheres

Wind Danger

Mt. Everest's peak is so high that it is in a jet stream. This means that the average winds at the summit are 190 kilometers (118 miles) per hour! Standing there is very dangerous. That's part of the thrill and challenge for climbers.

Ocean **currents** affect the weather, too. The Gulf Stream is a warm ocean current—a huge river of water in the ocean. It forms in the Caribbean Sea. It moves north along the east coast of the United States to North Carolina. There it turns and flows across the Atlantic. It helps to warm Great Britain. Without it, the weather in Great Britain would be like that of Siberia!

This is a satellite image of the earth from space. It shows ocean circulation. Ocean currents flow around the world because of differences in temperature and salt content in the water. A current of warm water (the red line) from the Pacific Ocean travels west. As it flows, it evaporates and becomes saltier. The Gulf Stream carries the warm, salty water up along the east coast of the United States and then toward Europe. At colder northern places, the water becomes so dense that it sinks to the sea floor and

Lab: *How Raindrops Form*

In this experiment, the bottom of the jar is the earth's surface. The warm water is water on the surface of the sea. The salt makes it like ocean water. The jar lid is high up in the atmosphere. The ice cubes simulate the temperature of the upper troposphere, the layer of atmosphere closest to Earth.

Materials

- $\frac{1}{4}$ cup hot water (not boiling)
- clean, dry clear glass jar with a screw-type metal lid (16 oz. jar is ideal)
- $\frac{1}{4}$ teaspoon iodized or kosher salt (not a reduced-sodium salt)
- 4 ice cubes
- cotton swab with two ends
- scissors

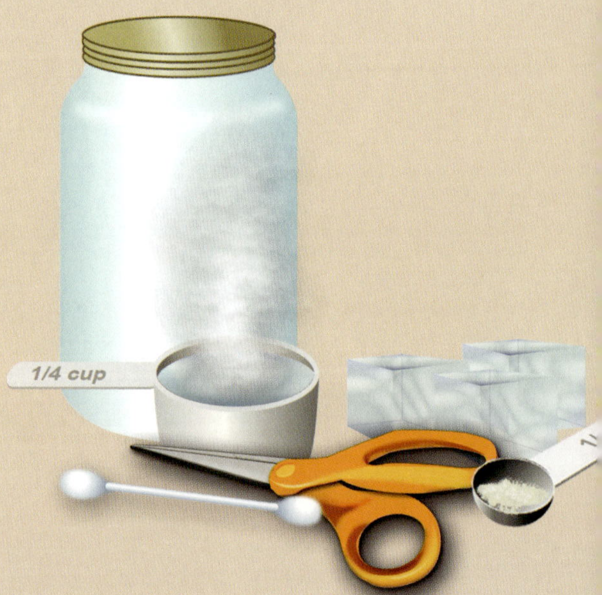

Procedure

1 Put salt into the bottom of a clean, dry glass jar.

2 Pour hot water into the jar. Stir the mixture with the measuring spoon.

3 Stick the cotton swab into the water. Taste it to be sure that it's salty.

4 Use scissors to snip off the used end of the cotton swab.

5 Place the lid upside down on top of jar.

6 Put four ice cubes on top of the lid.

7 Observe the underside of the lid after 15 minutes. Record what you see.

8 Use the cotton swab to absorb one of the drops condensed on the underside of the lid. Taste it. Record whether it tastes salty or fresh.

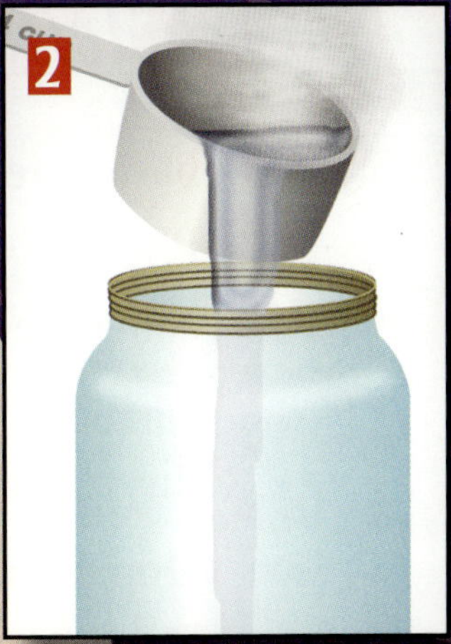

Conclusion

Water from the ocean evaporates into the atmosphere. It condenses when it rises high into the atmosphere due to the cold temperatures there. This condensation forms rain droplets. However, when water evaporates from the oceans, it leaves the salt behind. This explains why hurricanes form over salt water yet drop fresh water.

Glossary

barometer—an instrument used to measure air pressure

condense—to change state from vapor to liquid

current—a steady, smooth, onward movement and direction of water or air

Doppler radar—equipment that uses an antenna and radio waves to detect wind and precipitation

evaporate—to change state from liquid to vapor

front—a boundary between air masses of different temperatures

precipitation—liquid or frozen water falling from the sky

storm surge—tall ocean waves that arrive ahead of a hurricane and cause flooding near the coast

supercell—a large thunderstorm with a spinning updraft that can cause hail, damaging winds, and tornadoes

thunderhead—a tall, large storm cloud filled with moisture, electrical energy, updrafts, and downdrafts; may also produce hail

Index

Sally Ride Science

Sally Ride Science™ is an innovative content company dedicated to fueling young people's interests in science. Our publications and programs provide opportunities for students and teachers to explore the captivating world of science—from astrobiology to zoology. We bring science to life and show young people that science is creative, collaborative, fascinating, and fun.

Image Credits

Cover: Maxim Cherok SG/Shutterstock; p.3 Matej Krajcovic/Shutterstock; p.4 (top) Adrian Hughes/Dreamstime.com; p.4 (left) Shuttestock; p.4 (right) Photos.com; p.5 (left) Adrian Hughes/Dreamstime.com; p.5 (right) Jacques Jangoux/Alamy; p.5 (background) Photos.com; p.6 (top) Jostein Hauge/Shutterstock; p.6 (right) Kat Mack/Shutterstock; p.6–7 Kevin Norris/Shutterstock; p.7 Jack Dagley Photography/Shutterstock; p.8 (top) Jhaz Photography/Shutterstock; p.8 (bottom) Historic NWS Collection; p.8–9 Jhaz Photography/Shutterstock; p.9 Photos.com; p.10 Photos.com; p.11 Lou Linwei/Alamy; p.12–13 (background) Jim Zuckerman/Alamy; p.12–13 Tim Bradley; p.13 Topical Press Agency/Hulton Archive/Getty Images; p.14 (top) Igor Talpalatski/Shutterstock; p.14 (bottom) David Lewis/iStockphoto.com; p.14–15 Peter Arnold, Inc./Alamy; p.15 NOAA; p.16 (top) Historic NWS Collection/NOAA; p.16 (bottom) Peter Blottman/Shutterstock; p.17 NWS Collection/NOAA; p.17 (right) POPPERFOTO/Alamy; p18 (top) Mike Theiss/Jim Reed Photography/Photo Researchers, Inc; p.18 (bottom) Dainis Derics/Shutterstock; p.19 NASA; p.20 (top) Clint Scholz/Shutterstock; p.20–21 Dainis Derics/Shutterstock; p.21 Bettmann/CORBIS; p.22 (top) Ilya D. Gridnev/Shutterstock; p.22 (bottom) Getty Images; p.23 (left) Shutterstock; p.23 (right) Ian Jackson/AP Photos; p.24 (top) Marko Kovacevic/Shutterstock; p.24–25 Tim Bradley; p.25 (left) Ttphoto/Shutterstock; p.25 (right) Stock Connection/Alamy; p.26–27 Tim Bradley; p.28 (top) Paul Maguire/Shutterstock; p.28–29 Nicoll Rager Fuller